"It's all here, all the nuances of bo[...] poetic attitude. How flow became [...] again, the creative-growth-process of living writing—line breath before line break, a risk in every room. Tara Betts makes silence plea then whips some crazy and some natural on the confessional. Often sassy, often black-a-demic, her non-discriminating eye is never without a fully focused art-sense of self, community and nation. So many of the poems in *Arc and Hue* aim for the spirit level of insight, our need-some-more-saturation souls. No bragging, no cussin' folks out or refried allegorical posturing, *Arc and Hue* respects the currency of creativity and the unbought lives it honors."
—Thomas Sayers Ellis, *The Maverick Room*

"The poems in Tara Betts's debut collection, *Arc and Hue*, are a montage of identity politics, sexuality, music, and experiential knowledge. The joy of reading these poems is that it's the knowledge—yes, even more than the music—that makes these poems sing. Irrespective of how familiar the scene may seem on the surface, whether the focus is a reverie on relationships—some familial, some romantic—or a projection of a subjunctive future, the acute attention to detail and keen point of view guides Betts's work to conclusions that surprise and illuminate."
—A. Van Jordan, author of *Quantum Lyrics*

"Tara Betts' *Arc and Hue* is a banquet of sound. With rhythms sometimes jazzy, sometimes bluesy sometimes full of samba or bop, Betts' poems also cover considerable thematic ground, beginning with questions of otherness and 'hue,' the double bind of navigating the world when pale skin and straight hair 'deny brown coiled inside.' Betts' lyricism finds its lessons in legacy, history, experience and loss. To burn the master's house, these poems say, you 'need to kill it…not forget,' to raise your fists 'bare-knuckled, tangling with omission.' You need to sing the songs that 'burrow like wounds' and never stop singing."
—Paula McLain, author of *Stumble, Gorgeous* and *Less of Her*

"Tara Betts' deftly crafted stanzas are infused with a relentless lyricism and a Chi-town girl's sensibility. This debut collection solidifies her status as a defiant and singular voice, joyous indication of a fresh new direction in poetry."
—Patricia Smith, author of *Blood Dazzler*

"The poems in *Arc and Hue* speak from the spaces of the in-between and forgotten, spaces where only the most daring writers tread. Whether telling the story of growing up biracial in Illinois or the largely nameless victims of lynching, these poems showcase Betts's talents for musicality and formal play. It's almost as if the page itself shakes from the bass of the woofer and the treble of her speech. Betts makes no apologies about being black or female, and these poems don't flinch from the blue hues they paint. Hers is a necessary voice."
    —Susan B. A. Somers-Willett, author of *Quiver*

Arc and Hue

Tara Betts

Willow Books, the Poetry Imprint of

AQUARIUS PRESS
Detroit, Michigan
www.willowbookspoetry.com

Arc and Hue

Cover Art: "Gathering Series: Untitled #4"
by Makeba Kedem-DuBose
Cover Design: Sung-Hee Son
Author Photo: Rachel Eliza Griffiths

ISBN 978-0-9819208-7-0
LCCN 2009933916

Willow Books, the poetry imprint of
AQUARIUS PRESS
PO Box 23096
Detroit, MI 48223
(313) 515-8122
aquariuspress@sbcglobal.net
www.aquariuspressbookseller.net
www.aquariuspress.blogspot.com
www.willowbookspoetry.com

Printed in the United States of America
First Edition

for Dr. Lem D. Callahan, Charmaine Betts, and Bennie Betts, Sr.

"i wander regularly in moments of the dead/if you wd have me
speak/you must learn the tongue of my dead & loved ones/i have
been left behind/a survivor/holdin out for more"
—ntozake shange

"All these ships that never sailed/Today I bring them home/and let
them sail forever."
—T.S. Eliot

Contents

Foreword   9
Acknowledgments   12

I.

Housekeeping   15
Another Unwilling House   18
The Birth, Then Roses   19
Understanding Tina Turner   20
the darkest part   21
When I First Listened to Billie   22
when the uterus pleads   23
Arc and Hue   24
What A Crazy Aunt Can Give   25
Branching   26
Why I Collect The Hair   27

II.

Switch   31
What It's Like to Be a Mixed Girl   33
    (For Those of You Who Aren't)
Other People Like Me   34
Mapping Sketches of Spain   35
Dreadlocks   36
Lock Maintenance   37
Spent Imagination   38
when the men you love marry   39
The Answer   40
Neither One Says Goodbye   41
Call Me   42
When Love Is a Surgeon without a License   43

III.

Killed Twice   47
Slow Dance   48

States of Undress   49
Erasure   50
What the Well Provides   51
Venus Hottentot's Onlookers   52
Burn   53
Not On the Menu   54
The Burial   56
Microphone & Cotton Gin   58
Jena, Louisiana   59
Hurricane Kwame Offers His Two Cents   60
The Broken Levees   61
Sestina for the Sin   62
On the Digging Up of Emmett Till   64

IV.
Neruda's Email to Slam Poets   67
Astronomy Lesson   69
There Goes the Neighborhood   70
One More Chance   71
Tonglen Breathing in Detention   72
Don't Ask, Just Know   73
Block Party Speculation   74

V.
A Survey on Enjoying Verse   77
Proverbs from the Pulpit of Rev. George Clinton   80
Hips   81
The Vestal Virgin   83
Escape of Choice   84
Bowery   85
Corner Canzone   86
When Slumlords Don't Respond   88
For Those Who Need a True Story   89

Notes   91
About the Poet   93

Foreword

A Woman's Music Will Not Be Crushed

Arc and Hue is a house carefully built out of the poet's outreach to the world, feeling it the way hands do when they become our eyes, when touch composes the poet's song. Tara Betts' dazzling collection of poems speaks also to the need to take down houses we do not need, these structures where things that hinder and haunt us gather and make nests for themselves. Betts is a poet who is after a supreme structure, one that allows us to dance.

Standing inside her spirit, a woman comes to know the terrain of courage. Speaking her own narrative with names she chooses, a woman makes her own discovery of a love supreme, love of self, love for a just world, love for the unalterable singularity in the way the sun rises on any given day; taking these names inside the perfect orchestra of her heart, a woman connects to those who have gone before and stood up in the face of disorder and the dominant will of a world made of things that men most often imagine. These are the octaves of the music of Tara Betts, a poet who writes of taking the single locks in a lion's mane and giving them names. Betts establishes her own will to compassion in poems that ask why there are so many boundaries to caring, poems that are formed out of the genuine and not the veneers of self-seeking. This is a voice that has apprenticed itself to poets who write for the world and not to it, and in writing for the world she reveals her own world, a tandem motion of the hand on her own heart and on the heart of what lives outside her skin.

In the frame of an unabashed lyric narrative, Betts delivers poems that range in structure from a standard stanzaic to a more open field composition, with lines full of both subtle revelation and a deliberate dissonance to match the injustice she often takes as her subject. In poems such as "The Bowery" and "Sestina for the Sin," the poet writes out of the immediate space of injustice, recording wrongs as she sees them and offering them to the reader as an appeal. Writing of lynching in "Sestina for the Sin," Betts blends a lyric tension into a compassionate sweep as the poem's ending, writing that a sin "...refuses to explain the paring of flesh or air..." Her commitment is to art as the framework for upholding and refining our notions of goodness and our definition of what is human, and this does not come at the expense of her own issues. She is not a revolutionary without a personal life, but she also valiantly rejects the notion of mining personal issues of race and identity to form a careerist strategy. "A Survey on Enjoying Verse" is quintessential Betts, a poem still hot with the ink of a pen that is more sword than the tool of the scribe, more the just comeuppance than a gentle nod to nonsense.

In "What It's Like to Be a Mixed Girl," she has a definitive answer to the question of whether someone with a white parent and a black parent is white or black. The answer is final and definitive, as it configures the lines of her political concerns in the world beyond America's fascination with race. She writes, "it's dreaming your hair curls in proportion to/ your miraculously darkened skin, then/waking up when your voice reminds you/You're black."

In the title poem of the collection, Betts wonders "...if joy comes in small plastic buckets..." She is playing with her nephew, drawing and coloring. The poem is a settling into a moment, the lines finding their way into the memories, revealing layers of sensitivity in what we already know is a sensitive consciousness. It is the moment of a poetic engaged with the world in a way that is more important than many of us readers will acknowledge, and I would like to think this collection will gather in the energy of our consciousness and align itself with collegial forces, allies in the spaces in which we dream and hope, and there make itself felt, make itself known to us, to me more deeply and to you, who perhaps are reading the work of this wonderful poet for the first time.

Tara Betts is a poet who sees the prize as a world more firmly committed to a loving embrace of itself, and in that there is the beauty not only of a transcendent love but a poetry that rises above the conflagration of ego.

The arc and hue of Betts' aesthetic is an infinite compassion, where hope lives.

Afaa Michael Weaver
Beijing, China
May 31, 2009

Acknowledgments

So many brought me here. Thanks to Afaa Michael Weaver for his mentorship and Marilyn Nelson shining atop Soul Mountain. Thank you to the careful eyes, encouragement, advice: Christian A. Campbell, Aracelis Girmay, Randall Horton, A. Van Jordan, Raina Leon, John Murillo, John Rodriguez, Annie Finch, classmates and faculty at New England College, especially Anne Waldman, Alicia Ostriker, Paula McLain, Ross Gay, Issa Lewis, Truth Thomas and M. Ayodele Heath. For the literary families that made this book possible: Cave Canem, Acentos, Young Chicago Authors, Urban Word NYC, Malika's Kitchen and the Vineyard in London (especially Peter Kahn, Jacob Sam Larose, Naomi Woddis and Yemisi Blake). For your support and friendship: Tayari Jones, Latasha Diggs, Alexa Muñoz and to dear, dear Rich, and so many others who could fill a book.

I

"Truth-tellers are not always palatable. /There is a
preference for candy bars."
—Gwendolyn Brooks

Housekeeping

"I am a brick in the house that is being built around your house."
—Cornelius Eady

The house sprouts legs that leap when
no one's looking. It shakes me inside
like baby beads in a blocky rattle, cackles
and crows after sleep has rocked me gently
into a dark peace that its beams jar
with their whining.

I was looking for a small peace called
safe harbor, soft cookies and sun-dappled sitting.
I was looking for living room.
I was looking for cleanliness, shelter
and shelves to hold photo albums
this house spits on the street.

I pull on boots as the house caterwauls past
midnight. My flashlight clicks on a yellow eye
and casts its bright shadow on the spirit I thought
dead, the tradition that plagues my skin.
Howls of his favors pin glossy awards
to his chest. He has dripped his blood into the foundation,
smeared pipes with his grease and blended into
white walls, slightly pink at dusk.

I have been sitting in his house,
praying for a kindness wrapped in bows
that will never come. This house hoped
that I'd pick through its garbage. Its walls whisper
about collapsing to taste the powder of my bones.
The voice bounces within his doppelganger
rooted in lumber, concrete and steel. I make it
to the garage before he recites lines that

obliterate my sonnets and root me next to cotton gins.
The house exposes the lightest jezebels,
not just the darkest whores
who'd dare to straddle the canon.

The appropriate smell of oil does not disguise
the heft of the chainsaw, sledge hammer, drill,
hatchet. The rooms jump, laugh, taunt
with his superior couplets as I kick the door.
I want him to see this. He has to watch.
The kickback is not too strong when the saw's teeth
gnaw into the bedroom wall, chews
drywall clean through to next room.
Red welts prickle his arms.

I kick open the hole to the bathroom,
smash the shower doors, medicine cabinet
and toilet. His jaw cracks, but he is still
laughing. Until I raise the sledgehammer to the
dainty spigot that erupts in water and shattered
tile. This blueprint turned alter ego
holds his crotch, a new eunuch.

I have to kill the house, not forget it.
Break the tiny decorative windows
with a hatchet and start drilling
holes in floorboards and stairs
as we run to the door.
The knob sizzles with rules
insisting that I have to play along
to live, thrive, be happy.

I break it off with familiar
sledge hammer weight. The house
groans under the burdens of wounds.
What's left has the mercy of match

and gasoline to stop what began.
In the halo of the small flame, I calmly
remind this collapsing, almost charred place.
We choose where we live, if we can.

Another Unwilling House

Softened skin from salty sweat as lotion.
Flesh finds sparks for abrupt genesis when
cells race toward guessing games—daughter or son.
No money creases against debts contend-
ing with her copper hopes minted daily
with clock punch, grades and checks earned.
Latex tears its climactic finale.
Letters spelled CLOSED on her brain's lit screen, burned
a punctuated sentence and clamped shackles.

Each penny squeezed into her bank of dreams
squandered on uncommitted kisses that
lock her in, heave her beneath parent beams,
beyond blueprint, drafting her architect
sketches mother once wanted to collect.

The Birth, Then Roses

Samsara was snow that dark morning
when my limbs reached outside
my mother for the first time. Inches
of white frenzy blocking the road
to the hospital.

Whenever a bunch of roses appears,
it's my father in a hospital doorway
for my birth and then my brothers,
one of them not even his son,
bouquets of red in his hands.
My mother saved some petals in a book.
My petals have been piling
fantasies in my head ever since,
hoping to earn roses of my own.

How each red silky slip of flower body must have
brushed against my mother's face. Heavy sugar
to claim the carriage and birth,
not enough to coat pricks to come.
How the fists and philandering were unexpected.
How much sweeter it felt to hear the name
of her first child, a daughter, pulling away,
out of her, pushing a path into chaos that begins
them both.

My mother needed more than petals.

Understanding Tina Turner

Quiet girl found a voice mama could not quell
inside Nutbush City Limits. The baby
blasted beyond timid Annie Mae into Tina,
grind of muscle, hip, fierce calves
dominating heels into domesticity.

In the early music video era,
I soaked up her battered denim jacket,
leather mini-skirt, spiked wig and stilettos.
I'd throw my head back like her
rippling antennas of brown hair,
belting to no one in particular,
What's Love Got to Do With It?

Twenty years later, people joke
about Ike's fists granting Tina her name,
how she transitioned terror rooted
in spousal rhythm and blues to rock diva,
thunderdome warrior queen
with a mountain mansion overseas.

Hurts twang the womb
then escape into songs—like a man
who never holds you too close, too long,
trying to crush music within.

the darkest part

purple brown shaded into lips
brown unlike pink nipples some
suspect me of having.

darker woman's hidden signature
in flaps of skin concealed in hair
darker than paper bag.

enveloping brown kissed
thighs parted, toasted from
mouth to mouth.

When I First Listened to Billie

I needed an escape from the father's
knuckles. Our sprouting bean
uprooted when I left him like
a broken home that collapses
or gets half-mended. Her voice
softened cramping loss into blur.

I kept thinking *love is like a faucet.*
It turns off and on as I stood
in the shower with a new lover.

Instead of blood, a piece of tissue
thin as sliced ginger fell
from between my legs.
Arms steadied me on the tub's rim,
no clots, no life, just water
wetting porcelain.

when the uterus pleads

pink flora eases into
chaka khan's low command
tell me something good
dripping through lips like honey.

no sparks manifest flesh
knock on the door or ask to enter
when the bud cringes tightly
through night chills.

flesh petals—a fist that sings
cravings, a growl bent deep
between spine and hips
croons a siren song
hopes to lure some part
of him to a little death.

Arc & Hue

Jabari and I sketch with dust
from colored chalk—blue heads,
orange cars and trucks, lines from green poems
snaking down the hitched hip curving
just past the hedges to straight sidewalk
squares. My brother draws a son's head,
and I wonder if joy comes in small plastic
buckets with its silt coating my fingers
in soft indistinct pastel poofs
protecting each hand, each palm
glowing with deliberate lines rubbed
away with moist and breeze. This boy
will not remember his aunt's open hand
playfully pushing her brother, his almost father.
He will not notice how quickly arc and hue
crafted, turns to dust.

What A Crazy Aunt Can Give

The one sign that I am the crazy aunt
is that I keep envisioning the gift I want
to give to nieces when they start to sigh,
write long letters, or sneak off to horde
the phone, and wear the tiniest clothes.

Before they repel the clutch of elders
entirely, I slide the pink box across
the kitchen table. It is light, thin
cardboard suitable for confections
or pastries. The creamiest pink
silk ribbon wraps itself in lush bow
that unknots with one gentle pull.

Pink paper reveals the battery-powered
device, not huge with length or girth
but dainty as a lip gloss or butterfly.
I expect the horrified look, nervous
bursts of laughter, a storm of footsteps
tromping out the room, but the hope lingers
that she will take it.

This box opens the crazy
possibility that she can please herself,
then pick boys like a preference
for the most durable battery.

Branching

Jabari bobs and weaves closer
then away from me, this old aunt.
He darts toward adventures
paired with pizza, root beer,
read-me-a-story times.

Breathing in the green trees,
I ask Jabari to touch one.
Stand close to rough gray creases
branching out into full waxy
reflectors of the setting sun
that we walk closer to every day.

When he touches the trunk, he plucks
leaves as easily as tearing paper.
I stop his hand, tells him trees
may not walk or talk, but they breathe.

He yelps.
I inhale with a bittersweet smile,
take air I shared with my uncle
who resides where all trees go.

Why I Collect The Hair

Long glints of my hair
slither into soft bulk
tightly circled black cords
gripping each strand
that seems to hear you saying
leave them there nesting,
but I extract them delicately,
sometimes a dozen or more
because mothers cling to sons.

Years ago, a college boyfriend left my bed
 to go home. His mother honed in
on the brassy streaks
and pulled them off
with *what white girl are you seeing?*
So, I'm still plucking, gathering up
small tumbleweeds in my palm,
clues that deny brown
coiled inside me.

II

"…Our history is far stranger than you suspect, and we are not what we seem."
—Richard Wright

Switch

"Typical day that the black girl sees/comin' home wantin' more from a college degree." —Nas' "Black Girl Lost"

crushed zirconium gloss & glory
glides across her lips.   she looks
in the mirror, puckers, pops her gum,
knows what would
happen if mama saw her
       switch
               girl
bounce-bounce song scripts
pinned into rivets of denim
pressed into thighs rockin
two-pocket shorts cause she can
       switch
               girl
purveyors of pulp nonfiction
sit on regals wit chrome rims
mockin constellations
and damn her pelvic metronome
       switch
               girl
a poet sketches what he imagines
as her fantasies
behind his microphone
he pastes her into fables of blow jobs for hand bags
haphazardly stitches her walk into crack alleys
half-tapes her barely breathing body with bruises
       switch
               girl
women sit facing the microphone
their pupils spin full circles
the girl is each one of them
when she had the periodic table of elements

next to cut-outs from right on!
she wanted to be a nurse
or just get an A in chemistry quietly
while looking like
doing something she ain't
       Girl,
            switch.

What It's Like to Be a Mixed Girl
(For Those of You Who Aren't)
for P.S. & M.S.

well, i've got to say, it's people claiming
you're torn between tragic paths
when you know exactly where you walk
it's hair being pulled out by girls who see
stuck up high yellow bitch
stamped on your breath
it's brothers blurting
damn i thought you was white
then asking for your phone number
it's being painted with zebra stripes
with brushes that assume you're confused
it's classical & hip hop cymbals clashing
it's you & your brothers
calling each other 'nighonk'
because neither epithet fits
it's comparing yourself to
chocolate/vanilla swirl pudding pops so
you don't carry the weight of
in-between & enslaved fractions for names
it's your coworker's bottom lip dropping low
when you hang Audre Lorde's picture above your desk
it's recognizing a bass-filled moan
rolling into a phone's receiver from your mouth
it's questions, transitions, connections
it's tackling which hair moisturizer won't make
greasy clumps or itchy scalp with no help from momma
it's dreaming your hair curls in proportion to
your miraculously darkened skin, then
waking up when your voice reminds you
You're Black.

Other People Like Me

First she's saying *GD or Til The World Blow Up?*
The question loud enough to provoke looks
as the tin of the bus doors folds and closes.

She's looking at her friend with meticulous braids
no wider than corn tassles cultivated across her scalp.
These sisters got thighs and hips filling seats
like Sunday buffets. They are an overflow of *damn*
and *she-ain't-even-grown-yet*. The girl is no exception.

She never looks up at me, a could-be cousin.
Her dry hair broken at odd lengths
and escaping her pinch of ponytail spiking
up. My glance does not draw her attention.

The two girls loudtalk each other over passengers
between them—who got beat down and crisp peach
and blue stripes of a boy's button-up when he gets
on the bus. Pinch of ponytail notices the shirt.

She's said *nigger* at least five times
in cluster of faces like hers.

The braided friend begins *Don't say the n-word.*
That's what looks at me *other people call us.*
Suddenly, paler, hair too straight to need a perm,
not thick enough and carrying too many books,
in one glance, I've been pushed from the bus
that I've known since birth. I become *other* again.

Mapping Sketches of Spain

Your hands a soft heat
that cradles my chin.
My jaw rests in the crook
of your thumb, like holding
a pencil that loops and scrawls
landscape dense with doubt
against duende's father.

Jolts jump across
fingertips, balance
on bottom lip ledge
like Gibraltar kissing Morocco,
like Seville winking at the Atlantic.

There are swells racing
footfalls in my chest
as if Pamplona dressed
me in red despite bulls
running at us heavy,
but careful as flamenco
skirt turn or castanet click.

Sometimes, you admit
Miles pulls at you to sculpt
hips, waist, thighs, breasts.
My face mimics
Portugal while Madrid
and Barcelona fan out
into cities of my hair
across your pillow.

Dreadlocks

He lets me bury fingers in the lion's mane
longer, thicker than brown, tame waves around my face
delicate ropes spiraled from the same coiled, dark genes
sleeping in my recessive traits

Black, spongy tendrils
mimic shafts of light filtering
onto his back as sun bleached auburn

A man's hair never fell around my shoulders
and shielded me from city light clutter
never arched its tiny antennas in my direction
yanked a yelp from his head if I failed
to watch where my hands rested as I slept

Now, I want to count these boneless fingers
bending to tickle my cheeks and neck
I want to gather these battalions of thick delight
between my knuckles
grab each of these arms holding me close
and give every one its name.

Lock Maintenance

Rub brazil nut shampoo
onto palms. Add a little
tea tree oil so the scalp
sighs upon touch.

Rub soap and oil
into his scalp. Watch
eyes close like last night.
Work up the lather.

Rinse each fibrous gleam
til water runs sudsless.
Repeat as desired.

Massage hands with jasmine
oil and shea butter. Apply to
soft tufts rooting their way
out of skin. Remember
the hair needs it most.

Do not fear popping
locks apart, binding
them like old letters,
separating bunches into plaits
so you can play in his kitchen.

Twist at least 9 times
clockwise as if coiling
rungs to God.

Spent Imagination

index finger was
tip of his tongue.
another afternoon
tangles our limbs & hair,
eyes clamped shut
in the dark bedroom
with unzipped jeans
still on, still naked.

thumb turned into
corner of his mouth
my lips kept circling.
palms remember
his palms
holding hips
like the only
cradle rocked.

when the men you love marry

after they're gone, you are missing parts, diminished.
the shutter clicks on each of your parallel selves.
each one wedded to a different man in various stages
pregnancy, childbirth and mothering forged

into a steel trap, stopping you cold and bloody at the ankle,
no distance between pragmatism and swelling dream.
you grasp sheaves of poems wedged in crooked space
between floorboard and baseboard. you must do everything.

don't even look like you need help – webbed space to fall
and halt the crash of your spine. no life preserver
fishes you out of doubt, terrified by the plumping call
of a new body curled within that would

sink you, drown you, make you forget
your name and words twirling between your fingers.
these thoughts heap behind your eyes when they say
how smart she is, how smart she is…

The Answer

when an old lover asks if you're pregnant,
you want to offer the right answer
that cups you both gently.

his poker face would fold
if you said you swell with
fleshy hope. you wanted
that once with him.

there are no babies to fill the space
between. your body remembers
holding blood, a thick coat
of garnet and amethyst, nothing
sliced from inside, though
it would have been. picture
the knife extracting the growing
kernel spiting his unready fears.

he looks at you years later,
rocked by another pair of arms.
eyebrows cocked in recognition
of swing and balanced words
exiting your mouth, a slow sashay
dressed in smiles.

you can safely say no today.
speculation asks
if he had taken root,
would he have cradled you
in the valleys of calluses
and practical gestures,
running to the store, fixing
the broken bedroom light.

Neither One Says Goodbye

When the key jingles, her face crimps.
The lock resists turn, push, release,
mirrors her taut goodbye lips.
Listen, Gladys Knight & The Pips.
Neither one wants to break the lease
but someone has to flatten first.
All buoyancy deflates, flickers
like her words were muted by curse.
He will try to persuade, bicker
to bedroom. She closes her purse.

Call Me
A Bop for the Bowery & Chicago's Wicker Park

When bills crisper than bread crust
deny faded and distressed cache
like denim ripped intentionally
pretending to be worn by time,
who's first in line to agree to interviews?
Some veterans insist.

Call me (call me) on the line. Call me any, anytime

As if Blondie's voice still flirts with hip hop
in overt sampling and identical strip malls.
At least the texture of filth makes a street
where each footstep stamps a signature.
Each rat a glyph on a scroll that goes unread
until rodents become memories glazed
so children who want sips of the city
drink safely and remember a chorus belting
call me (call me) on the line. Call me any, anytime

When a place becomes landmark
it is lost on the map of once was.
Hints of the former self waver
their mirage in photographs,
and journalists pen quick articles
to sell copies, imitations of an original.

Call me, call me on the line.
Call me, call me any, anytime.

When Love Is a Surgeon without a License

Trace teardrop from narrow tip to wide bottom

Left to right   Right to left

Toggle middle switch blur

Work into nonchalant figure eights   skate delicate fingerprints

Too hot to touch slice of vinyl pie cradling
                    sonic nostalgia against eardrum, posit touch
                    like a lover who knows
                    what spot   when to slide
                              stop

        so breath held is a given, then released scream.

Flip the record.
Crackle pop hiss passst mint condition
Grit don't kill the song any more than dirt muddies
true heart unless you had no heart in the first place.

        Push past

        Whoosh aah whoosh   *whoop tweaka*
REWIND take it back!
        Under palms of life revisited.

Bloom fresh cuts.
Heal without scars.
Songs burrow like wounds
sing on cold, damp nights.

43

Look for records breaking
open like a maggot brain.

Records take you home again
where sweat did not irritate,
sneakers were not immature,
what was heard sounded pulse
because the roof is always on fire
unless you put it out.

III

"come celebrate with me that everyday something has tried
to kill me and has failed."
—Lucille Clifton

Killed Twice

Before the chubby-cheeked age of ten
I knew death could breathe on you early.
Another little girl who spelled her name
same as me was found in a drainage ditch.
Adolescent claws bled a life out of her.
I never forgot same age, same name.
Twenty years later, I am watching
television with my mother in bed.

The same teen, now a man set free
finds a tow-headed boy a few blocks
from the drainage ditch years past,
then loses him, the boy just a body
when found.
His elementary picture blazes innocent
across the screen, but the local paper
front page imprints plaits,

twisted black cotton candy
wrapped in pairs of purple plastic
bubbles, square teeth smiling
singed, semen traced
on what's left. Brown skin
turned ash and bone.
She could have been me.

Slow Dance

after Kerry James Marshall

The wrinkled pants and undershirt,
a worn copy of last month's Ebony magazine
can't cover deliberate etchings of Erzulie's heart
on my living room's yellow table. I lay out
a plate of asparagus drizzled with honey
after I light the candle corking a red/black bottle.
Then prayers bend through speakerbox.
Wisp notes snake through vintage quiet storms
at the midnight hour when Elleggua's eyes smile
towards a gold Venus. I tell gods from every corner
about my plans. Kneel on a rug ringed with Oya's
rainbow petticoats. The knock at the door
swings an adrenaline fist through my chest.
Now, Betty's dress, a sliver of banana peel,
pressed against this rumpled offering of me.
Her wide eyes are the sweetest closed doors
tonight. Her head never leans
into the niche of my collarbone.
She wonders what brought her back.
She thinks it's the pale rouge of roses
riddling the air. She will never know
I begged powers older than Jesus,
more desperate than escaping the crucifix.

States of Undress

His voice deeper than riverbed booms "flash
me." Every piece of clothing shields what's underneath—
goosebumps rise across yes, blushing flesh
circles her bones with memory wonder
that insists he enter. *Please be her guest*
stepping into the foyer, shudder-arc
of bodies buckled together, suggest
some things are done anytime, light or dark
when moon whispers what's written by Lorca,
words tensile as untainted layer of snow
breaks underfoot while zipping parka.
Silence makes them bother curious below
the body's veneer—so temporary and weak.
They both need to button, fasten and speak.

Erasure

Every face slowly dropping out of the world
like they never had breath, laughter or tears.
Chunks of history scooped out of the book of life,
burned for kindling, tossed into landfills
buried in chips from obsolete computers.

Too many bodies have been drawn
into centrifugal black holes, never to be seen
before they come clearly into view.

There must be some weathervane willing
to announce a shift in the wind.
There must be a gust of hands willing to turn
the rooster's iron head away from absence.

History is pulled from my mouth
slow as a string of pearls, one bead at a time.
I stock the shelves with more substance than
porcelain figurines. I am raising my fists,
bareknuckled, tangling with omission.
Or it is an embrace caught again and again
between my fingers.

What the Well Provides

after Maxine Hong Kingston & Nicole Cooley

Found her at the bottom of the old well
where her death by drowning proved genuine.
No sleepwalking accident, curse or spell
thickens the well water fattened sanguine
with wasted red, a necessary hex
that carried all her troubles and goods,
organs connected to her swelling sex.
Bloated flesh, now pale, chilled and leaking blood.
Her iron flooded the well with power
distilled into deep pores of the well's stones.
Discovery opens eyes to death hour.
Clabber of rope rings bucketless knell tone.
Trying to escape a child's weight, she bore sweat
that carried much more than she thought she'd get.

Venus Hottentot's Onlookers

Loud with primal curves, her posterior must be
some trait for adaptation or mating. Clothes cannot
contain such an oddity. Let's pay so we can stare,
for centuries. Her daughters will be paid to shake
for music. Send her dead ass back to Africa
after we've put her labia in formaldehyde
and we've counted our money. Ass is all that's worth
seeing here. This mark of the whore, savage sex caught
in a labyrinth of steatopygia. I want to keep looking
at this zoo on two legs.

Burn
(Oak Park, Illinois, 2005)

Imagine eyes green as peeled grapes,
loose black curls frame baked brown
flesh. Her eyes hint at the Irish
that led her to high school
classrooms plusher than segregation.

Her words construct towers
of light heated with fuels
distilled from confrontations.
Mother spears dark daughter
with epithets everyday.

The school officials say she
won't be back. Imagine, she
burned her house to the ground.
She was living H. Rap Brown's
fantasy screaming *Die, Nigger, Die*

with a match.

Not On the Menu

If Portugal was edible, could it be swallowed
like some country fruit, goosebumped as unripe
avocado, heavy with sweet guava wet that lingers?

Would Africa taste bitter and glitter
on tongues with its ripe diamond seeds?
Would the silt of India be the truest curry
bursting a heat against the mouth's roof?

An international hors'doeuvres platter
crosses tourist imaginations like
a hectic maitre'de. There are
Indian families in steamy kitchens,
Taiwanese men's bicycles crisscrossing
Manhattan's traffic-glutted streets,
Puerto Rican girls smiling for bigger tips
when offering mofongo and Cubans
proffer mojitos and freshly killed chicken
for that one night at El Hueco.

America, though, would distance itself
from its bitter Billie Holiday image in stalls
of worldly produce. America would be slick
with campaigns on its nutritional benefits.
America would be so shiny the shellac needs
cracking and peeling. America's fruit,
so sweet it eats teeth with its ache.

While movies ripen into
culinary pornography
Eat, Drink, Man, Woman,
Soul Food
Tortilla Soup
Like Water for Chocolate

The cinematic menu sounds
like a veil pulled across the face,
the sweaty thump of samba,
a pinprick protruding
from a map of exotica
where the spare grain
of days remains unsampled
since the trees of America
require so much tending.

The Burial

The Wife
We crossed the threshold
that Henry'd laid with his own hands.
With each step, the church got smaller
so I held tissues in my gloved hands,
wiped my face til the tears drew up.
My fingers stayed damp.
Henry always loved my hands. He'd come
with his cracked paws dusty and tough from bricks,
lumber, nails and the till, then gently brush a stray
hair off my neck. He'd wash under his nails.
In the deep trails of his palms, dry them and coo
into baby girl's face while tickling her soft new tummy.
Never thought I'd see the day
when other men would carry him,
heavy enough for three men and Bible verse.

A Pallbearer
Lucille was what you call solid to the bone.
Even her tears couldn't muddy that. I knew
when she was fifteen that there was nothing
but clean corners, laundry lines and eyelets of fresh
white curtains winking from the shine of her brown eyes
crying today. It's a damn shame. She's clutching memories
tighter than my grip on this casket. Part of me hears
her tinkling young girl laughter fluttering against my chest.
I never told her.

The Priest
Precious Lord, buoy me on the raft of your scriptures.
There are some truths that are the only ones we need.
Lucille missed the shadows of her husband's shoulders.
I knew them chapter & verse.

I've been holding the pot of everyone's whispers.
I'm burying my one sorrow, a pot licked clean.
Henry, I pretend to tell the living, take my hand.

Microphone & Cotton Gin

Blues dressed in satin
already been traded and sold
between microphone & cotton gin.

Can't find no balance, yang nor yin
or hear tales old bluesmen once told.
Blues dressed in satin

mean another song done gone, been taken.
Ain't never been a thief more bold—
snatch everything 'tween mic & cotton gin.

Can't untwist fabric into bolls again,
can't unpress records the bluesmen sold,
now blues dappled in satin
dropped in the devil's collection tin.

Past rhythms thrown to tailspin
no longer sweet talked but cajoled
bluesmen bought with dollars. No satin
poured into microphone, another cotton gin.

Jena, Louisiana

for Robert Bailey, Jr., Mychal Bell, Carwin Jones, Bryant Purvis,
Theo Shaw, Jesse Ray Beard

Noose turns epithet.
Slurs, a bread that rises
into red leap. Southern
heat thaws time, drains
the school of race.

Parent whisper is criminal & cry.
Hell is ajar as prison door.
Stunt entertains pale slap
to cinch brown boys,
ebb their hope, woo their murder,
shatter them in airless cells,
stamp mothers with ash & shade.

Lawyers must win, stop the pyre
with brothers for timber.
No one's a slave, raw as history's rope.
Who raises the stone of conspiracy
pressed down on sons?

Pitbull paws will score their
chests unless we jeer, swarm
around the shawl heavy as steel.
We become new sum where
three times two is one.

Hurricane Kwame Offers His Two Cents

My sister Katrina just twist-whipped the Big Easy.
She wanted to see how stone cold bitch she could be.
You know, us hurricanes don't start off as giant
funnel cakes rolling houses and trees in sweet death.
We're usually just some restless stirrings,
rustling waves like fluffy baby locks
blowing across the Atlantic's head.
You could say our rotating relatives
were Africans, born on the continental coast.
Of course, our cousins from the Pacific come
mostly from South America & Mexico, but
those Olmec heads look a lot like faces back home.
Katrina can't front that they were making too much
zydeco/jazz rumbling saturated with gin and hoodoo.
Even God understand a party every now and then.
All them loas just like Jesus.
These reverends preaching cleansing have no idea
how close hurricanes curl toward the ears of God.
In fact, my girl Rita decided to visit Texas just to rattle the faith
of that president boy's skull, that brain of his clattering
around like a mess of dried beans. These journalists lack
just as much sense talking about people looting,
well hell, I must be one of Nature's looters snatching
from whatever these newspapers call Civilization.
Ain't it human nature to eat, drink water and diaper a baby?
At least one journalist got it right though, spelled
my name correct and e'rything. He said this Hurricane
should have been called Kwame or Keisha, but still,
I'm not so sure that was a compliment, since some
hold African names they don't like,
so tight in their jaw, you'd think someone still
made up names for chattel, like unmarked
graves wishing that the family bible remembered them.

The Broken Levees

You were not built to last, not like Ninth Ward
dwellers who recall waves swelling, churning
against your feeble back. Your spine hardly held
the muddy flesh and wetlands blood.

White plastic bracket, corrugated steel
cowering like cardboard under water's fists.
There must have been some guilt, regret, maybe
a sense of inferiority when you opened, simpering
like some neglected sagging gate.

You knew you were not up to this.
Military men shallowly planted you,
an undernourished wall, not wide
nor tall enough. Your vitamins were fear,
oil, Mardi Gras tourism, voodoo and jazz.

You should not be blamed,
child pressing your will against Mami Wata.
No thumb in the dyke could stop the flow.
None of your idiot engineer fathers spoke ethics.
They simply did their job and sent their weakest
out to be plowed like a field of homes and families.

Mended, made the same, not enough for Katrina
or categories climbing past two. Whisper to those
staking your bones and patching your wounds.
Murmur about cacophonous crash and scream.
Tell them about the scent and taste of dying.

Sestina for the Sin

Executions don't always occur in the dark.
Picnics with children in daylight's open air
as families await a lynching,
a preoccupation whetted by social habit.
Rapist or too damn uppity, some would explain.
One of these, the victim's sin.

Who committed the sin?
The question presses heavy and dark
as spilled blood no one can explain
as white families take in humid air.
This appreciation seems curious habit
when they hope to stifle wind with a lynching.

A little boy reaches for a man's ring at a lynching.
Lacking fear and reverence for the dead marks his sin.
His parents encourage this habit.
While Black children are pushed into the dark
away from the burning stench flattening air,
parents hide brown youth, unable to explain.

No one can explain
lost head, missing limbs, burnings, a lynching.
Silence intercepts air.
Sometimes, discovered bones document sin,
brittled and festering in the dark,
an endemic trait of this habit.

Concealing tokens of guilt identifies habit.
Daylong celebrations fail to explain
why murderers step out of the dark
when they grin at the rising rope of lynching,
sanctioned sin,
when cheers and fading screams puncture air.

After victims have no use for air,
rituals gather around this peculiar habit.
Picking through the bones becomes part of the sin.
Crowds face cameras to explain
This is what happens at a lynching.
This is what happens when you are dark.

A sin obscures dark reason, refuses
to explain the paring of flesh or air
when the gruesome habit is lynching.

On the Digging Up of Emmett Till

Backhoe disturbs grass, unburies the gore.
What might be left of once young Emmett burst
open as a kicked-in, splintered door.
No autopsy but mother saw her curse.
Nothing left of her coppery sunshine
after his bout lost in night's arena.
No hand drawn smiles or cut-out Valentines,
just some acquitted laughing hyenas.

Rumors still insist he couldn't have been
the long ago crumbling balloon of flesh.
He walks around still sweating off his gin
where grain distilled turns drink, mash threshed.
If this body isn't Emmett unearthed,
isn't he son, a Black child of some worth?

IV

"...like amnesiacs//in a ward on fire, we must/find words/or burn."
—Olga Broumas

Neruda's Email to Slam Poets

From: cantogeneral@gmail.com
To: info@slampoetry.com

I greeted the falcon of death when
Allende sunk like a familiar battleship.
The glass, once crystal seabirds, fell across
my invaded floors in cherry, lime and watery
fragments.

My salvation was like Matilde's
warm breath nestled in the shawl
of pulse and memory.

My name scattered in poems,
black silkworms of love letters
scrawled on the wooden fence
outside my home—
a utopia christened Isla Negra.

The people remembered this baptism
of words that caught their lives
like so many fishermen's nets, like
the toucan's beak wet with sips of
rainbow catching an eye.

The people said my poems were
necessary bread, fireplace specter,
a loving hammer against fear.

So, I ask you if ink on a napkin matters
when bullets dare you to approach a fence,
write simple phrases, tender as tilapia,
like *love you. miss you. Recordamos.*

Please set the wayward pigeons
of your words free if they will not make
bread, provide dry shelter, or mend a fence.
Please respond to stomachaches that require
more than beer-soaked ego when the points
they know best belong to bullets.

in love,
P.N.

Astronomy Lesson

The language of stars rings
ancient sprays of laughter into
plots beyond axis. Light smashes
into arcs yet distance lies about
how close it comes to our eyes.
The largest sack of torn marbles
scattered with deliberate astronomy
offering the oldest calendars.
The plans of every moment mapped
and looking down at our small dust
lives, the tangos between
birth and death. This skin
blanketing day's end glistens,
and we have been taught to fear it.

There Goes the Neighborhood
for Maxine Kumin

Aerial shot omniscient view bent above
asphalt playground. Sidewalks become
concrete football fields where Brooklyn
accents weigh down boys' tongues
that count like girls circling one another.

They bend clothesline, extension cords,
double helix style rotations beneath
spinning jumping sneakers.
Speakers turned walls claim
the street as official block
party bidness. Metal drums split
open with orange charcoal guts plead
for red meat, then sizzle relief.

Brownstone stoops fill with girls
clinging to gossip like the new neighbor
holding his golf club bag as if announcing
shift change for baggy pants & oversized
shirt-wearing boys who stand too long on
the corner. Count each baby in mad math
that's called living. Take a breath when
change claims one more before you blink.

One More Chance

for Faith Evans

What happens when summer thickens
with notorious rhymes from Bed-Stuy,
when pulse quickens
heavy as thumping bass deep-fried?

There is a laying of hands on cheeks
more sincere than any bullet.
A chorus of chambered muscles speaks
in red tandem pairing. A trigger pulled
fires our lips and skin into one long streak.

My eyelids shudder then blink.
He's trapped in this delicate dance
too. I nod and think
when the widow chanteuse sings,
baby, gimme one more chance.

Tonglen Breathing in Detention

This older woman, long skirt, practical sandals, a professor
with benefits and theories, tries to convince me to inhale suffering,
take in mold trapped in brick walls, scowls from faces
that insist that I will tell their secrets to parole officer, attorney
or psychiatric evaluator who could give a damn about a single
brown, poor or young face inside this brick and locked doors.

I try to explain to her how my shoulders immediately slump
into a smattering of bones jumbled under my skin, and knots
that pile up where my neck meets my shoulders when the door
clicks its final grimace into the lock. The lights dim
as I head toward classrooms guarded on all four corners.

She does not see the translucent paper of my lungs growing heavy
with mucus in this place, or the cavities of my head congested
with toxins oozing from skin, mildew, dripping sewage.
The trapped feeling reminds me that I can go home in a few hours.
This is just a job, just a place that warehouses young bodies before

they graduate to penitentiary. Some days, you breathe deeply and watch
the dangers race toward your nostrils like refugees from Pandora's Box,
springy, hairy with bulging eyes and charging to overtake me
in a slow, inevitable implosion. I wonder where they might
leak out of this sorry sack of bones. They giggle upon exit toward new hosts.

I'm lying on the crumbled corners of water-damaged linoleum,
deflated, hearing the march of sneakered feet unlaced tromping
in lines around the regimented square of hallway. All the morning
faces I saw are still accounted for there, before I deplete
sips of air that spraying sage and peppermint oil in water permits.

Don't Ask, Just Know

A friend's bright blonde afro during
the family Christmas party declared
an awkward holiday—stiff jaws

wedging silence between father and son.
His outing an obvious bubbling beneath
the skin, reaching the awaited boil.

He called me for escapades with house music
and Janet Jackson bending blackened
warehouse walls of The Generator.

Sweating and red on the dance floor
without meat hooks aimed at my skin,
except for one woman, I ducked

into a room swole with men in work boots.
Carhartts, overalls without shirts.
We gathered a crew in the cold.

Golden Nugget Pancake House
in all its diner grease glamour
was the final stop before families

reclaimed us in the sweep
of a New Year. We ordered
our starches of choice.

Under the dim lights, we checked
our silverware, but the only spot
I noticed was a dark brown scab

the size of a pinky nail
balanced on one eyebrow.
I already knew not to ask.

Block Party Speculation

Heat waves roll their pulse across exhausting
avenues well worn by solar trolley.
Midday sunlight welcomes bareskin trusting
despite water's lack and sunburn's tally.
Needle drops. *"Can I borrow a dollar?"*
Nod to the record while narrowing eyes
sidestep when bass-shaken stance might holler.
She licks lips flavored blackberry surprise,
walks like her steps match low beats on djembe,
pepper pot singing degrees of how hot
her shimmy might be. He needs yohimbe
root, ginseng and vitamins in his pot,
brewing courage steeped in beats not quiet.
Shy masked with slick—his usual diet.

V

"It is always the love that will carry action into positive new places, that will carry your own nights and days beyond demoralization and away from suicide."
—June Jordan

A Survey on Enjoying Verse

Use a No. 2 Pencil only.
Make solid marks that darken your response and your mood.
Do not use ink, ballpoint or felt tip pens in any color.
You must not enjoy filling out this survey in various hues.

For the first 7 questions, please fill in the response which best corresponds to the canon which does not include you and performance poetry that believes in sexy, bad language. Interpret the three previous adjectives—performance, sexy, and bad—as you will.

1. In the past week, how many times have you been asked to purchase titles that have not been spellchecked?
2. If clichés were offered daily during meals, how often would you lose your appetite?
3. If you purchased at least one drink at a pretentious club and/or open mic, were you nauseated or too drunk to remember any of the poems?

If you heard poetry, did you listen to it at one of the following places? Please mark YES or NO next to 4. through 8. (If you did not listen to any poetry, please skip to question 9.)

4. Alone in a smoky bar while wishing your sorry ass lover would take you back.
5. At a poetry slam since that's how you get to go on tour and hawk the CDs you just burned and the chapbook with your picture on the front.
6. At a respected literary organization or conference so academes, publishers, and editors know you're a REAL poet.
7. At a jazzy nightclub reminiscent of the Miles Davis album cover for *Kind of Blue* or the video for the digable planets' 1994 hit "Cool Like Dat."

8. Bobbin' your head in the freestyle cipher because you need that hip hop/spoken word adhesive to make it stick.

The following statements are regarding poetry. Please tell us if you agree or disagree with each statement.

9. Listening to poetry makes me seem sexy or cultured.
10. Reading other poets might influence my work.
11. If you think there are poets of color that we professors need to read, then tell me, who should we read?
12. There are no women writing anything worth listening to.
13. Poems are supposed rhyme, right?
14. Somehow the postmodern paradigms have been transmogrified by these mongrelized attempts at formalist structures that avoid narrative constructs through nonlinear inventions that deconstruct our understanding of language.

We are interested in your knowledge regarding poetry. Please respond True, False or Unsure to the following.

15. I have read at least four Pulitzer Prize-winning poets.
16. The only two poets I know are Maya Angelou and Langston Hughes.
17. Poetry is low in agent-hungry fat.
18. Poetry may contain some pesticides and cliché residues.
19. Some poems suffer from over-workshopping.
20. The Environmental Protection Agency and Food and Drug Administration agree with Gil Scott-Heron that poetry will not make you five pounds thinner.

We would like to know your reasons for not buying poetry. Please indicate the answers that correspond most closely with your excuse.

21. I couldn't find the poetry section at the bookstore, much less the book.
22. I can read it on the internet.

23. I used my money to buy the latest urban classic *PimpHand: Smack Them Hoes Wit Love.*
24. You want me to read something?
25. I write it and I don't make enough money to buy a damn thang. Wanna buy my book?

Proverbs from the Pulpit of Rev. George Clinton

The kingdom of heaven is within.
Never underestimate the power of ass.
Get your daily allowance.

Science fiction ain't fiction.
Our father who art on Wall Street
and with the FBI make it so.

My Cadillac and pinky ring restore me
when unwashed armpit & strawberry incense
saturating the block cannot.

Yea, though I walk through the shadow
of poverty, I seek the boogie in booty.
The ass always follows the mind.

Hips

the bony projection of femur
known as the greater trochanter
the overlying muscle and fat

everything in the known universe

comprehensive, open-minded,
uncensored human interactive
proofs, an attempt to bring
humans back into the picture.

heavy tribal belly dance
forcing a 'bunker mentality'
designed to end the cycle of abuse
of sex workers on the streets,
work with them to improve
their lives and give them tools.
hips direct, swivel all-female.

original groovy, funky, jazzy area
on fire salsa, merengue, bachata,
bolero, bolero son, cumbia
dance hall. be heard, not scene.

live it safe. prevent breakage
fractures are breaks in the thighbone
just below the joint. most require
hospitalization and surgery.
prop them up afterwards.

dizzy circus professional
hoola hoop stuntperson
houdini didn't have these.

homage. they need space.
go mamasita, bellydance,
yoga, hand dance, samba, salsa!

uncertainty, guardian fury,
inspectors protest.

what about your hips?

The Vestal Virgin
after Giovanni Battista Moroni

The miracle of me, unbroken
seal on the letter to lust.

My palms balance this sieve
fingertips stroke its wide brim
chiming with waters inside.
It holds firm as ice
that never melts or spills.
Touch the sides and bottom.
Dry as marble.

The folds of my gown falling
like tender sacraments
between my legs, spread only by me.
Glances collect at my thighs like coins.

I cock my head while dreams
of translucent pink nipples
dissolve into the white sand of me.

Oceans shift, denying lunar demands.
Waves gather momentum under pressure
until I wonder how much I can hold.

Will I be as porous as a bowl punctured,
unprotected by chastity, destined
to wonder what leaks from inside?

Escape of Choice

She swelled at two months
like red print of a slap
beating a rhythm on her face.
He offers his fist instead
of groceries, and she knows
this can happen more than once.
She has contracted. She has eased.
This is a lost baby poem.

He does not stop her from working,
taking out the garbage, going to class.
He does let her find a random condom
wrapper, snatches the phone from her,
ignores her open arms and laughs
at another bill.
No one admits this is wrong.
No one sees her leave or stops her.
She has contracted. She has eased.
This is a lost baby poem.

She comes back empty,
ready to fill her bags,
exit the guilt shattered by blows
with no beginnings except this one.
She runs out the door, escapes
one plot for her body.
She has contracted. She has eased.
This is a lost baby poem.

Bowery

Once, it was fistfuls of angry teeth and lovelorn needles
mocking bright plumage fortified
by Elmer's Glue and aerosol neon.
Peeling rock posters still crumble anarchy
for young pierced rebellion looking for
more than a T-shirt. Young peacocks fan
bright feathers over cleaner streets.
No bums perch in the doorways unless you
count black men crouched on steps of the shining
sliver of a building that still has vacancies,
including the absent NO LOITERING sign.
The syringes stubbed on concrete have been trashed,
sterilized and handed out again. Catholic Workers
sit with legs wide in front of open windows
two blocks down, but the wood panels nailed together
block the view of demolition.
This fence turns crystal ball for onlookers
forced to polish their futures. Warning:
Prostitutes crossed suicide's ledge here.
Children became interior designers of cardboard here.
Rats have been crushed only to linger on tenement air.
Frayed corners are being trimmed with brightly lit
boutiques, but the unfinished hem hangs loose in places.
Sweet sour redolence clings to concrete baseboards, and dusty
history book pages detail each New York street, peeling away.

Corner Canzone

He swallows huge gulps of air
hunts for brighter light,
a sign of life like air.
The cold frosts the spectral air.
After running inhales ache,
he wonders when warmer air
will fill his lungs still craving air
constantly like a steady burn.
Without pure air nothing can burn,
not even the troubles that he wants to air
like shooting speeds of a freed star
unpinned from indigo with other stars.

He once tried to count each star.
which is like trying to count air,
but he found comfort in a star
that shined hanging on his neck, a small star,
tiny replica of distant light.
He hoped one day he'd be a star.
Yeah, find his own Walk of Fame star
without walking until his feet ache.
He wanted to crush his needy ache
that pinched in his chest and burned.
He forgot fame is fading, it burns

a spectacle, bright, too fast of a burn
at times, crashing meteor, wasted star.
No one follows the aftermath of burn
unless there's currency & flash bulbs to burn.
He hopes, in ignorance, for plush scented air
that costs more than cigarettes he might burn.
He thinks he's unable to burn
on his search for a timeless halo of light.
He remembers searching for honeys under strobelight

Women so sweet the feeling lingered like a burn,
but he does not want to lose the ache.
All he wants to remember is the ache.

He'd give it all up for the ache,
but there are no sensations without cash to burn.
So he stood in the cold with full pockets and bones full of
ache.
Winter winds made his eyes tear, not heartache.
He thought he could rock mics, maybe be a movie star.
He just asks, "Are you straight?" if someone has an ache.
Every fiend has to answer to their ache
as if it is able to inhale air.
Being poor hangs over you like smog painting the air.
While the hopeful street pharmacist aches
for his chance to blaze under the spotlight.
He did not expect sirens or red & blue lights.

He never thought about the price of light
unless he paid mama's electricity, a responsible ache
trapped in his bones like X-ray light.
He kept wondering when he'd study sunlight
without watching his back or hearing popping sounds burn.
He was tired of pushing weight when he wanted to be light
wanted to escape like flying Africans toward clouds, light
sun, homeland, heat, moon, stars.
If Spike Lee make another movie, he wants to be the star.
He just didn't know how close he was to light.
His pocket packed with paper that might as well be air.
Money seems like it ain't real, but it's there, like air.

He thought this in his last gasps for air.
His red soaking through snow & moonlight
where he feels what never felt like an ache.
He shakes with a shivering burn,
a hole trapped in his skin like a purple star.

When Slumlords Don't Respond

At first, the ceiling opens up a crack
of relief, as if an old woman's skin gasps
under layers of slathered foundation.

When it writhes across the ceiling a few
more inches, calling the landlord
and pouring yellow water
from a plastic pail shapes daily ritual.

Caked-over patchwork plaster strips
fall from the growing hole. It haunts the
room with gurgle echoes at night.

After two months, the hole opens like
a parted labia, a rich brown at its center
pouring liquid amber that can't be mopped
up any longer.

Crumbled ceiling lines bucket bottoms.
Bathroom leaks weep, while talking
to the distant empty room.

For Those Who Need a True Story

The landlord told Raymond's mother that twelve dollars
would be deducted from their rent for every rat killed.
She sends her son to the store for a loaf of Wonder Bread
and five pounds of ground beef. Young Raymond returns
with bread and meat that she tears and mixes inside
a metal bowl. Mama seasons this meatloaf with rat poison
pulled from the cabinet beneath the sink. Well done,
meat sits steaming in the middle of the kitchen floor.
Then the scratching scurries. The squeaking begins
and screeches toward the bowl.

Raymond describes the wave of rats like a tidal crash
covering the bowl, leaping over each other's bodies,
then the dropping, the stutter kicks.

A chorus of rat screams rambles through Raymond's ears.
Keening, furry bodies tense paws against churning guts
as they hit cracked linoleum until an hour passes.
Silence swept away the din in death's footsteps.
The mother's voice quivers in her next request.
Raymond, help me count them.

They waded through these small deaths with rubber gloves,
listened to the thump of each dead rat as it rustled against
the slackness of plastic bags.
Raymond wanted to stop counting,
but Mama needed to save a dozen dollars
wherever she could
if they wanted to finally leave the rats behind.
After the last rat was counted, Raymond handed
the bag to the landlord as proof. Here.

Enough rats to skip the rent for three months.
Enough rats to avoid the fear of sweet sleeping
breath leading to bitten lips.
Healthy children wrapped in designer dictates
cannot describe Raymond's fear of rabies,
the smell of poison rotting from the inside out,
the scratching inside the walls at night.

Those children
should find soft lives
that drop pendulums in their dreams
and never tell another story
about the ghetto
until they've had to count rats
with their hands.

Notes

The following poems have been published in the publications noted below:

OCHO #16: " Housekeeping" and "Hips"
Letters to the World: Poems from the Wom-Po Listserv (Red Hen Press): "Another Unwilling House"
Temba Tupu! (Africa World Press): "What A Crazy Aunt Can Give," "Killed Twice" appears as "The Little Girl Like Me Killed Twice"
RainTiger.com: "Bowery," "Call Me," "Why I Collect The Hair," "Hurricane Kwame Offers His Two Cents"
Callaloo and *Home Girls Make Some Noise* (Parker Publishing): "Switch"
ROLE CALL (Third World Press): "What It's Like to Be a Mixed Girl"
Reverie: an earlier version of "Mapping Sketches of Spain";
Bum Rush the Page (Three Rivers Press): "Dreadlocks"
Cave Canem VIII (Black Classics Press) & *Essence*: "Lock Maintenance"
Cave Canem X commemorative series: "Neither One Says Goodbye"
Ninth Letter: "Microphone & Cotton Gin"
MiPoesias: "Tonglen Breathing in Detention," "Slow Dance", "Other People Like Me"
PMS (poemmemoirstory): "Erasure"
WSQ: "Venus Hottentot's Onlookers"
labloga.com: "Not On the Menu"
Ninth Letter: "Microphone & Cotton Gin"
Aunt Chloe: "Jena, Louisiana"
November 3rd Club: "Neruda's Email to Slam Poets"
Black Arts Quarterly: "One More Chance"
Fingernails Across the Chalkboard (Third World Press): "Don't Ask, Just Know"
TorchPoetry : "A Survey on Enjoying Verse"
Hanging Loose: "Proverbs from the Pulpit of Rev. George Clinton"

WombPoetry: "Escape of Choice"

Hurricane Blues (Southeast Missouri State University): "Hurricane Kwame Offers His Two Cents"

SAY WHAT: "Sestina for the Sin"

Pluck!: "The Broken Levees"

Gathering Ground (University of Michigan Press) and *Spoken Word Revolution Redux* (Sourcebooks): "For Those Who Need a True Story"

About the Poet

Tara Betts is a lecturer in creative writing at Rutgers University in New Brunswick, NJ. She is a Cave Canem fellow who has received her residencies from the Ragdale Foundation, Centrum, Caldera and an Illinois Arts Council Artist fellowship. Tara is also a poetry editor for *November 3rd Club*.

Tara's work has appeared in *Obsidian III*, *Callaloo*, *PMS*, *Columbia Poetry Review*, *Ninth Letter*, *Hanging Loose,* and *Drunken Boat*. Her work is anthologized in several collections, including *Gathering Ground* (University of Michigan Press), *Bum Rush the Page* (Three Rivers Press), *The Spoken Word Revolution* (Sourcebooks), *Power Lines* (Tia Chucha Press), *These Hands I Know* (Sarabande), *Hurricane Blues* (Southeast Missouri University Press), and *Letters to the World* (Red Hen Press).